A YEAR OF US

Love each other with genuine affection, and take delight in honoring each other. - Romans 12:10

Happy Valentine's Day!
Shirley & Aaron

A COUPLE'S JOURNAL

We love you two,
Momma Dad

A YEAR OF US

One Question a Day to Spark Fun
& Meaningful Conversations

ALICIA MUÑOZ, LPC

ZEPHYROS
PRESS

February 2022

Interior and Cover Designer: Jamison Spittler
Art Manager: Karen Beard
Editor: Pippa White
Production Editor: Erum Khan

Illustrations © Sanny Van Loon, 2019
Author Photo: Tim Coburn

ISBN: Print 978-1-64152-424-7

To Mike

the ultimate co-adventurer
in past, present,
and future questions

Introduction

This journal is an invitation to be curious, to explore, and to share with your partner, every day for 365 days. With a daily question, it will guide you to connect with each other through memories, hopes, thoughts, dreams, viewpoints, preferences, flights of fancy, and your own unique essence. And it will allow you to focus on what turns you as individuals into the collective *you*.

If you already know each other well, this journal will strengthen your bond by giving you a daily touchpoint. If you are still getting to know each other, these questions will help you on that journey. No matter where you are in your relationship, using this journal consistently will help establish a *Love Ritual*,[1] which is a healthy relational habit that can replace unhelpful, defensive, or counter-dependent habits, and contribute to creating sustained happiness in a couple.

Each question has been crafted to generate self-reflection, activate your imagination, and awaken a sense of curiosity and play. The space that follows can be used for a brief answer or to jot down notes. You can use this journal in a variety of ways—with different colored pens to differentiate your notes, or you can alternate who asks and who answers the question each day. On very busy days, you can write your responses separately and then share your reflections whenever it's convenient for both of you. No matter how you choose to use the prompts, the goal of this journal is to foster conversation and engagement with each other beyond the page. (For this reason, the writing space is intentionally limited.) Ultimately this journal is a tool. It's here to beckon and tempt, and to encourage you to flirt, laugh, deepen, and honor.

The Year-Opener Reflection will help you and your partner set goals and intentions. The Year-Closer Reflection provides an opportunity to integrate what you've learned and appreciate how you've grown together over the course of your *Year of Us* journey.

The 365 questions you'll encounter loosely fall into these four categories:

 Future goals/dreams

 Play/sexuality

 Past/present

 Philosophical/ psychological

Each question is color-coded and is paired with one of the four icons so you can gauge at a glance the gist of the reflection for that day. This will help you decide if you're both in the mood to dive into it, or whether you'd prefer to skip ahead to a different category (and backtrack later to the skipped question).

The Austrian-born philosopher Martin Buber once wrote, "The world is not comprehensible, but it is embraceable: through the embracing of one of its beings."[2] Learning about each other in small, consistent doses is one way of embracing each other, and it will lead to the deepening of your connection.

---

[1] For more on Love Rituals, see my book *No More Fighting: 20 Minutes a Week to a Stronger Relationship* (Emeryville, CA: Zephyros Press, 2018).

[2] "Martin Buber Quotes," BrainyQuote.com. Retrieved January 20, 2019, www.brainyquote.com/quotes/martin_buber_386705.

Year-Opener Reflection

You and your partner may want to take a moment to reflect on where you are right now in your relationship. How would you like this journal to support you? How do you envision it enhancing your connection in the year to come?

Maybe you have specific goals, like learning more about each other's desires, practicing being present, or listening without judgment. Or maybe you just want to have more fun together. Get clear with one another about your expectations and the approach you'd like to take. You may agree on a specific time limit and on things you can do to stay focused and receptive before completing the daily question, such as silencing your phones so you won't be interrupted.

Taking time to reflect and make your motivations conscious will steer you in the direction of your relationship goals. In a year's time, you'll be able to return to this reflection page as a way of gauging where you were at the start of this process, and to appreciate how you have evolved as a couple over the course of creating this journal.

Here are five questions to help clarify your expectations for this journey:

1. What will be easy for us as we use these questions to connect daily?

2. What might be an obstacle?

3. What do you hope to get out of creating this *Year of Us* with me?

4. What can I do to help make sure we have fun doing this together?

5. What behaviors of mine might help you feel heard as we go through the questions?

In the couples counseling I do, partners get clear on their *intention* at the start of a session. What you'll be doing here—answering thought-provoking questions—isn't the same thing as therapy, but it's still important to align with your intention. Remind yourselves why you're doing this. Is it to grow as a partner? To learn? To connect more deeply? Aligning with your intention before sharing can help your responses come from a heartfelt place. This alone can help your partner hear you better.

As you go through the questions, pay attention to the specific wording. For example, "Is there something about you that I take for granted?" is *not* the same as asking, "In what ways do I treat you badly?" Hold an image in your mind of your partner *at their best* as you share and listen, and notice when you have an emotional reaction. Do your best to use the more probing questions to tread new paths of accountability together.

No matter where you start as a couple, I promise that by question 365 you'll have gained a more detailed, specific, and intimate sense of who your partner truly is—and possibly also of who you are.

1 DATE: _____

What's your idea of a special weekend together? Why?

_____

_____

_____

_____

_____

_____

_____

_____

_____

2 DATE: _____

What are the words you would most like
to hear me utter about you in my sleep?

_____

_____

_____

_____

_____

_____

_____

_____

3 DATE: _____

What famous storybook or movie character did you relate to most as a child, and how did it reflect your inner struggle at that time in your life?

4 DATE: _____

If you could be totally absolved of something you regret, what would you ask forgiveness for?

5 DATE: _____

If you had $150,000 to create a space that was all your own, and you could set it up any way you want, what features would it have, and why?

_____

_____

_____

_____

_____

_____

_____

6 DATE: _____

If we were to take a how-to class together (cooking, wine tasting, dancing, art, knitting, learning magic tricks, financial planning, podcasting), what class would you want us to take and to what end?

_____

_____

_____

_____

_____

_____

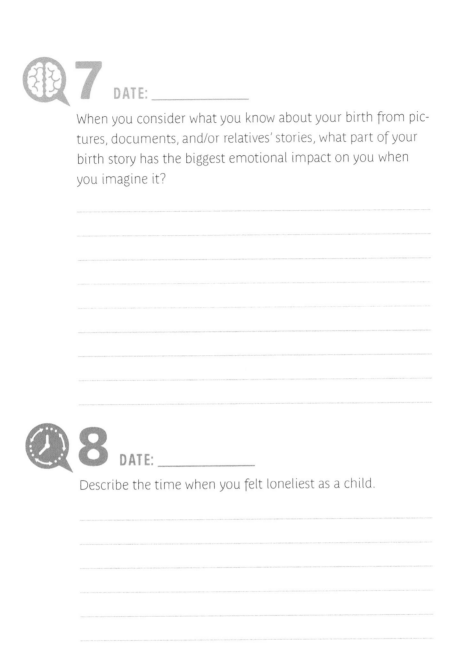

Q7 DATE: _____

When you consider what you know about your birth from pictures, documents, and/or relatives' stories, what part of your birth story has the biggest emotional impact on you when you imagine it?

Q8 DATE: _____

Describe the time when you felt loneliest as a child.

9

DATE: _____

What do you desire most for me, for yourself, and for our relationship in the year to come?

10

DATE: _____

Can you remember and share with me one of the first times when hearing your own heartbeat impacted the way you thought or felt about being alive?

11 DATE: _____

If cloning technology advances, and scientists are able to bring back an extinct animal, which animal would you want brought back, and why?

_____

_____

_____

_____

_____

_____

_____

_____

12 DATE: _____

Is there something about you that I take for granted, and if so, how might I show you I appreciate this more than I do now?

_____

_____

_____

_____

_____

_____

_____

_____

_____

Q13 DATE: _____

What might be different about you or your life if you no longer felt regret about your answer to question 4?

_____

_____

_____

_____

_____

_____

_____

_____

_____

Q14 DATE: _____

Can you remember one random act of kindness a stranger directed at you recently? What effect did it have on you?

_____

_____

_____

_____

_____

_____

_____

_____

_____

15 DATE: _____

What's the gist of a heartfelt letter you might write to someone with whom you're not speaking right now?

_____

_____

_____

_____

_____

_____

_____

_____

16 DATE: _____

A hundred years from now, when a monument is built in your honor, describe in detail the "quintessentially you" act that's immortalized in marble or bronze.

_____

_____

_____

_____

_____

_____

_____

_____

_____

Q17 DATE: _____

Have you ever had a gut feeling that you followed which led to something wonderful or protected you from something unsafe?

_____

_____

_____

_____

_____

_____

_____

_____

_____

Q18 DATE: _____

In an alternate universe, if you were born as the parent you had (or currently have) the most trouble with, what do you think you-as-them would need to be a better parent to yourself (e.g., self-love, wealth, safety, therapy)?

_____

_____

_____

_____

_____

_____

_____

19 DATE: _____

If you're on social media, how has it expanded you as a person, and how do you think it has impacted you negatively? If you're not on social media, why not?

_____

_____

_____

_____

_____

_____

_____

_____

_____

20 DATE: _____

If we and another couple got stranded on a remote island with no chance of rescue, which of our couple friends do you think we could get along with best, and why?

_____

_____

_____

_____

_____

_____

_____

_____

21 DATE: _____

If you and I decided to get matching tattoos, what would they be, where on our bodies would we get them, and what would they symbolize about us? If we *already* have matching tattoos, what's one thing we can do to manifest the deeper meaning of our tattoos in our lives?

_____

_____

_____

_____

_____

_____

_____

22 DATE: _____

Have you ever learned something from someone who held a political viewpoint that was radically opposed to your own? What did you learn?

_____

_____

_____

_____

_____

_____

_____

_____

23 DATE:_____

What is the wildest, most extravagant adventure
you can imagine us going on?

_____

_____

_____

_____

_____

_____

_____

_____

24 DATE:_____

What's an affordable adventure we could take, and what do
you think has stopped us?

_____

_____

_____

_____

_____

_____

_____

_____

_____

25 DATE: _____

What is something you envy about people who identify as a gender that isn't the one you identify with?

_____

_____

_____

_____

_____

_____

_____

_____

_____

26 DATE: _____

If the house were burning down and you could rescue three things purely based on sentimental value (not practical stuff like your phone, wallet, computer, etc.), what would you rescue and why?

_____

_____

_____

_____

_____

_____

_____

27 DATE: _____

Write a list of your current top ten "favorite things" in 60 seconds, then go through the list and tell me why you value each thing you wrote down.

28 DATE: _____

Five years ago, where did you hope you would be now? How has your idea of who you are and what you want changed since then?

29 DATE: _____

If you could single-handedly raise $1 million through a charity drive campaign, what cause would you support, and why?

_____

_____

_____

_____

_____

_____

_____

_____

_____

30 DATE: _____

Who would be on your Mount Rushmore of timeless favorite musical artists, and why? You can pick no more than four.

_____

_____

_____

_____

_____

_____

_____

_____

_____

_____

31 DATE: _____

Describe an area you want to grow in psychologically or spiritually.

_____

_____

_____

_____

_____

_____

_____

_____

_____

_____

32 DATE: _____

What's a recent embarrassing situation you were in, and how did you handle it?

_____

_____

_____

_____

_____

_____

_____

_____

_____

33

DATE: _____

What historical or future era, at any geographical location in the world, would you want to visit, and with what purpose or goal?

34

DATE: _____

Have you ever had a recurring nightmare or superstitious fear? What dilemma, need, or longing do you think it was connected to?

35 DATE: _____

What specific spiritual or religious beliefs resonate most with who you are at your core? If none do, why not?

36 DATE: _____

If you created a perfume that released a magical scent that could change behavior, what would you like it to make us do to create an unforgettable evening?

37 DATE: _____

What's the most important belief you want to teach or want others to teach today's children, and why?

_____

_____

_____

_____

_____

_____

_____

_____

38 DATE: _____

What was the most formative event in your life, and how do you think it impacted you?

_____

_____

_____

_____

_____

_____

_____

_____

39 DATE: _____

If I were going to pamper one part of your body that is not an erogenous zone for 10 minutes straight, what would you like it to be, and why?

40 DATE: _____

If the Internet shut down, electricity stopped working, and gasoline ran out, what survival challenges would be the hardest for us to overcome?

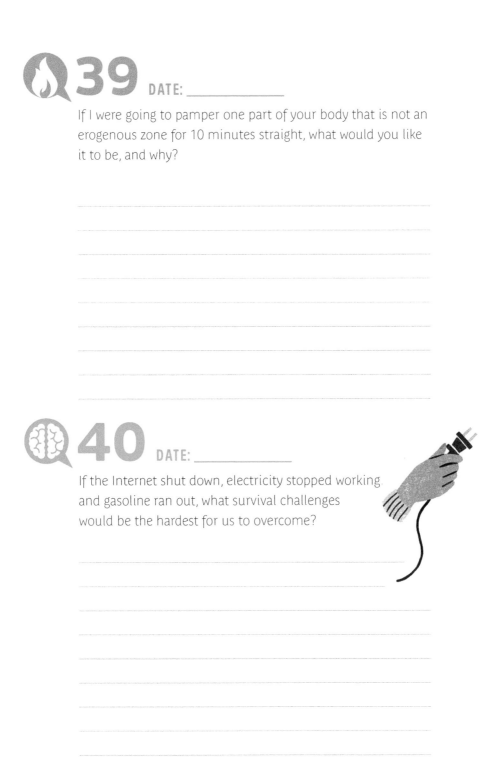

41 DATE: _____

How do you think our different skill sets would increase our chances of survival in the situation from question 40?

42 DATE: _____

Do you have a hobby or interest that you would love to get paid for? If so, what is it? If not, what would you choose if you could choose anything?

 **43** DATE: _____

Can you share an emotional memory centered
on your favorite childhood toy?

_____

_____

_____

_____

_____

_____

_____

_____

 **44** DATE: _____

Would you rather be a famous athlete or a famous artist/
creator of some kind? Why would you choose that type of
fame? What would be the pros and cons?

_____

_____

_____

_____

_____

_____

_____

45 DATE: _____

Describe your ideal wedding experience—either as the one getting married or as a guest at someone else's wedding.

_____

_____

_____

_____

_____

_____

_____

_____

_____

46 DATE: _____

What is something you've forgotten that you wish you could remember (or remember better), and something you remember that you wish you could forget? (Such as, "I wish I remembered how I felt before my first day of high school.")

_____

_____

_____

_____

_____

_____

_____

_____

 **47** DATE: _____

You have to spend 24 hours with your nemesis *or* 24 hours with *my* nemesis. Which would be harder/easier for you, and why?

_____
_____
_____
_____
_____
_____
_____
_____

 **48** DATE: _____

If you had the chance to enjoy one neglected body part of mine for 10 minutes straight, what part of me would you choose, and why?

_____
_____
_____
_____
_____
_____
_____
_____

49

What do you doubt most about yourself that most people think you're confident about?

_____

_____

_____

_____

_____

_____

_____

_____

_____

50

Have you ever had a supernatural (or supernatural-ish) experience, and if so, how did it impact you at the time?

_____

_____

_____

_____

_____

_____

_____

_____

_____

51 DATE: _____

Tell me about a powerful moment in your life when you overcame a fear or did something despite being afraid to do it.

_____

_____

_____

_____

_____

_____

52 DATE: _____

What would your time capsule to your future self say and/ or contain to remind you of the most important elements of who you are today?

_____

_____

_____

_____

_____

_____

_____

_____

53 DATE: _____

If you won $5 million in the lottery, what's the first thing you would buy?

_____

_____

_____

_____

_____

_____

_____

_____

_____

54 DATE: _____

Do you think your self-concept would change if you owned the thing you imagined buying with your lottery winnings in question 53? Why or why not?

_____

_____

_____

_____

_____

_____

_____

_____

Q55

DATE: _____

Can you think of a time that someone may have actually given you a gift by failing you, disappointing you, being selfish, or betraying your trust?

_____

_____

_____

_____

_____

_____

_____

_____

Q56

DATE: _____

If you and I were the last people left on earth, do you think we would value our lives more or less?

_____

_____

_____

_____

_____

_____

_____

_____

_____

57

DATE: _____

What foreign language do you wish you spoke, and what would you gain from learning it now?

_____
_____
_____
_____
_____
_____
_____
_____
_____

58

DATE: _____

What stress reliever do you currently rely on that could harm you in the long run?

_____
_____
_____
_____
_____
_____
_____
_____
_____

59

DATE: _____

In your own words, what's your view of the origin of the universe?

_____

_____

_____

_____

_____

_____

_____

_____

_____

60

DATE: _____

If there were one word or phrase you hear people say a lot that you could remove from the English language, what would it be, and why should it be removed?

_____

_____

_____

_____

_____

_____

_____

_____

Q61 DATE: _____

What do you like most about the way we
handle our conflicts?

_____

_____

_____

_____

_____

_____

_____

_____

_____

_____

Q62 DATE: _____

What historical event do you wish you could have witnessed
firsthand, and why?

_____

_____

_____

_____

_____

_____

_____

_____

_____

_____

63 DATE: _____

What's the most important thing you learned from your mom or mother figure?

_____

_____

_____

_____

_____

_____

_____

_____

64 DATE: _____

What's the most important thing you learned from your dad or father figure?

_____

_____

_____

_____

_____

_____

_____

_____

_____

65 DATE: _____

Would you rather have too much of a good thing and get sick of it or never have quite enough but always want it?

_____

_____

_____

_____

_____

_____

_____

_____

66 DATE: _____

If you could plant a tree that could grow anything, what would it be, and who or what would the tree and its "fruit" help? (The tree can't grow any form of money.)

_____

_____

_____

_____

_____

67 DATE: _____

In stressful moments, if you could freeze time and teleport anywhere in the universe to calm down and think for one hour, where would you go?

_____
_____
_____
_____
_____
_____
_____
_____
_____

68 DATE: _____

What's your favorite part of being the gender you identify as?

_____
_____
_____
_____
_____
_____
_____
_____
_____
_____
_____
_____

69 DATE: _____

What right now excites you—either about the path you are on professionally or exploring one of your passions?

_____
_____
_____
_____
_____
_____
_____
_____
_____
_____

70 DATE: _____

If you could discover and name a new constellation after me, describe how the stars would be configured and what you would call the constellation (it can't be my name).

_____
_____
_____
_____
_____
_____
_____

71 DATE: _____

Is there a hardship you've seen a family member or friend go through that they handled well and that you deeply admired?

72 DATE: _____

How do you think *you* would have coped with the hardship in question 71?

73 DATE: _____

What animal do you think embodies your personality the most, and why? What about mine?

74 DATE: _____

What do you honestly think about masturbation? How has your view of masturbation changed or evolved over the years?

75 DATE: _____

Describe your ideal day from morning till night.

_____

_____

_____

_____

_____

_____

_____

_____

_____

76 DATE: _____

How would you describe your relationship to your own orgasm: distant, close, or BFFs? How has it changed over the years?

_____

_____

_____

_____

_____

_____

_____

_____

77 DATE: _____

Do you think there's a difference between trust and faith? Do you trust life, have faith in it, neither, or both?

_____
_____
_____
_____
_____
_____
_____
_____
_____

78 DATE: _____

What characteristics in me do you most admire, and in what ways do you think these characteristics also exist within you?

_____
_____
_____
_____
_____
_____
_____
_____
_____

 **79** DATE: _____

Imagine waking up one morning into the exact same life you have now except that what you've always considered to be sexually "normal," "good," or "right" is suddenly seen by everyone else around you as "abnormal," "bad," or "wrong." How would this impact your sense of self?

80 DATE: _____

What field do you think is most important to the future of our planet: science, art, medicine, technology, psychology, political science, engineering, or something else, and why?

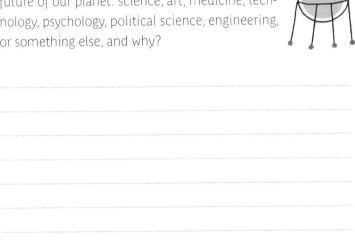

81

DATE: _____

What would you do with your free time and attention if you didn't have your phone, tablet, or any other type of technology for a day (besides trying to get a new one)?

_____
_____
_____
_____
_____
_____
_____
_____

82

DATE: _____

Describe the pros and cons of your most visible or most socially valued talent or skill.

_____
_____
_____
_____
_____
_____
_____
_____
_____

83 DATE: _____

If you were required to have a quotation on all your digital devices as a screensaver, what would it be? Would it serve as a personal reminder, as a bit of inspiration, or to let others know something about you?

84 DATE: _____

Name three important things, big or small, that are on your "must do" list for this year.

85
DATE: _____

Describe your least visible and least socially valued talent or skill and how this talent uplifts you.

86
DATE: _____

What do you see as the difference between self-care and self-ishness, and which one do you struggle with most?

87 DATE: _____

Describe what you think is my most visible or most socially valued talent or skill.

_____
_____
_____
_____
_____
_____
_____
_____

88 DATE: _____

What is one quirk about me that you were skeptical of at first but have come to love?

_____
_____
_____
_____
_____
_____
_____

89 DATE: _____

Describe my least visible and least valued talent or skill and why you think it's important.

_____

_____

_____

_____

_____

_____

_____

_____

90 DATE: _____

If you could write a book, what would it be about, and would your motivation for writing it be personal or financial? (If you have already written a book, choose another creative medium—film, painting, etc.)

_____

_____

_____

_____

_____

91 DATE: _____

Tell me about the most formative moment you had with an important teacher or mentor growing up.

92 DATE: _____

What do you see as the upside to periods of intense self-centeredness, or the downside to feeling too consistently connected with all of life and the cosmos?

93 DATE: _____

What's been one of the most transformative or meaningful moments you've experienced with me since we've been together?

_____
_____
_____
_____
_____
_____
_____
_____

94 DATE: _____

Describe one thing you long to accomplish in life to feel like a success.

_____
_____
_____
_____
_____
_____
_____
_____

95 DATE: _____

If you could create a new system of government, what would it most resemble: a democracy, a socialist government, a benevolent dictatorship, or something else?

_____

_____

_____

_____

_____

_____

_____

_____

96 DATE: _____

What words are you most afraid of hearing from a person in a position of authority?

_____

_____

_____

_____

_____

_____

_____

_____

_____

_____

97

DATE: _____

Would you rather commit an untraceable, "harmless" white-collar crime that makes you rich or prevent a crime that brings you no financial gain but turns you into a local hero and endears you to others?

_____

_____

_____

_____

_____

_____

_____

98

DATE: _____

Imagine we're lying in a meadow at night under a starry sky and we see a shooting star. What good omen might you interpret it to mean?

_____

_____

_____

_____

_____

_____

99 DATE: _____

What was a very special meal you once had, and why did it mean so much?

_____

_____

_____

_____

_____

_____

_____

_____

_____

100 DATE: _____

You have a choice between two superpowers: flight or invisibility. Which would you choose, and why? How would your new power affect me?

_____

_____

_____

_____

_____

_____

_____

_____

101 DATE: _____

How do you think the race and/or ethnicity you identify as may have led to either advantages or obstacles?

_____

_____

_____

_____

_____

_____

_____

_____

_____

102 DATE: _____

What's the most common characteristic you envy in people, and why?

_____

_____

_____

_____

_____

_____

_____

_____

_____

103 DATE: _____

When you make mistakes, do you feel like it's okay or do you struggle with shame?

104 DATE: _____

How has knowing me changed the way you think about love?

🔥105 DATE: _____

If you could create a scratch-and-sniff sticker that took you back to one of your happiest moments, what would the smell be, and why?

_____

_____

_____

_____

_____

_____

_____

_____

106 DATE: _____

How could we reconnect more effectively when we get stressed out or anxious?

_____

_____

_____

_____

_____

_____

_____

_____

_____

107 DATE: _____

Describe a strong, inexplicable (potentially even spiritual) connection you've felt to a place, thing, plant, or animal.

_____

_____

_____

_____

_____

_____

_____

_____

_____

108 DATE: _____

Is there an object or a way of being that you lost as a child that might move you to tears if you reconnected with it today?

_____

_____

_____

_____

_____

_____

_____

109 DATE: _____

Describe the closest thing you had to an imaginary friend growing up.

_____

_____

_____

_____

_____

_____

_____

110 DATE: _____

You have one magic penny you can throw into a wishing well and your wish is guaranteed to come true. What do you wish for in *this* moment, and why? (You can't wish for money.)

_____

_____

_____

_____

_____

_____

_____

_____

111 DATE: _____

If you could create a new language that would improve our communication, what would it be called? Why would it help us? What would you say to me right now in your new language?

_____

_____

_____

_____

_____

_____

_____

_____

112 DATE: _____

What sex education do you wish you'd received as a preteen or teenager?

_____

_____

_____

_____

_____

_____

_____

_____

_____

113
DATE: _____

What part of your cultural inheritance have you sidelined, struggled with, or seen as "less relevant" to your identity? How might embracing or exploring this aspect of yourself help you grow into a more whole, integrated, or complete person?

114
DATE: _____

Name the first special song that comes to mind when you think of love. Why is it special to you?

115 DATE: _____

Why do you think you like breaking or following rules?

_____
_____
_____
_____
_____
_____
_____
_____
_____

116 DATE: _____

Who was your first memorable crush, and why did you like them?

_____
_____
_____
_____
_____
_____
_____
_____
_____

117 DATE: _____

What is one painful thing you might be lying to yourself about (or in denial about), and why do you think it's hard to fully face or accept this particular truth?

_____

_____

_____

_____

_____

_____

_____

_____

118 DATE: _____

What simple activity could you and I engage in when we're feeling bored, low, or anxious that might help us feel more energized?

_____

_____

_____

_____

_____

_____

119

DATE: _____

What food or meal represents your childhood most, and what does it evoke?

_____

_____

_____

_____

_____

_____

_____

_____

120

DATE: _____

Can you take two minutes to write a haiku (five syllables/seven syllables/five syllables) about the best things in our relationship? (For example: "We laugh together/So seriously silly/Better than coffee.") When you're done, read it to me slowly.

_____

_____

_____

_____

_____

_____

121 DATE: _____

What would you like to pull out of a time capsule from your youth and reminisce about? Can you imagine doing it now with me?

_____

_____

_____

_____

_____

_____

_____

_____

122 DATE: _____

To you, does money most represent love, freedom, luxury, security, respect, or something else? How did this association evolve?

_____

_____

_____

_____

_____

_____

_____

_____

123 DATE: _____

Imagine you are the project manager creating the ultimate Pleasure Palace. What types of pleasurable activities would a visitor find in the rooms?

_____

_____

_____

_____

_____

_____

_____

_____

124 DATE: _____

What are some of the most obvious ways you and I are similar?

_____

_____

_____

_____

_____

_____

_____

_____

_____

_____

125 DATE: _____

What are some subtler ways we're similar that most people don't notice?

_____

_____

_____

_____

_____

_____

_____

_____

_____

126 DATE: _____

If I'm mad at you, what's the secret to expressing my anger in a way you can hear so I don't bottle it up and grow resentful?

_____

_____

_____

_____

_____

_____

_____

Q127 DATE: _____

Which of your relatives or early caregivers do you resemble most, and how?

_____

_____

_____

_____

_____

_____

_____

_____

Q128 DATE: _____

What influential person in your life did you rebel against that you've since come to appreciate, and in what way?

_____

_____

_____

_____

_____

_____

_____

_____

_____

129 DATE: _____

Imagine we were handcuffed together for 24 hours. Describe in detail what the hardest part of that would be for you.

130 DATE: _____

In your ideal home, what is the view from the bedroom window, and how would it make you feel to wake up to that view every morning?

131

What do you think would be the most difficult daily routine for me to give up?

132

What's one of your earliest memories?

133

If you and I produced a short film together, what kind of a film can you imagine us making, and what roles would we have in the film production?

134

What friend really understands you most of the time? How do they show their understanding?

135 DATE: _____

If I could wave a magic wand and take
away one of your major worries, what would it be,
and how do you feel when you imagine that worry
vanishing?

_____

_____

_____

_____

_____

_____

_____

136 DATE: _____

If there was one question you could have answered through
a dream, insight, or mystical experience, what would that
question be?

_____

_____

_____

_____

_____

_____

_____

137 DATE: _____

Please brag shamelessly about one of your most selfless or generous acts.

_____
_____
_____
_____
_____
_____
_____
_____
_____

138 DATE: _____

Is there something you're ashamed of now that you can imagine looking back on in five years and being proud of?

_____
_____
_____
_____
_____
_____
_____
_____
_____

139 DATE: _____

Can you recall and describe the moment you first suspected I was attracted to you?

_____

_____

_____

_____

_____

_____

_____

_____

140 DATE: _____

What's the single sexiest thing I could spontaneously do in your presence?

_____

_____

_____

_____

_____

_____

_____

_____

_____

_____

141 DATE: _____

What have you learned about the relative value of appearances over the course of your life?

_____

_____

_____

_____

_____

_____

_____

_____

_____

142 DATE: _____

What kind of affectionate touch or words of praise did you receive growing up, and how did it feel back then to get it or not get enough of it?

_____

_____

_____

_____

_____

_____

_____

_____

143 DATE: _____

How did I make you feel special, loved, or cared for today?

144 DATE: _____

Describe a photograph of you from an earlier time in your life that makes you cringe when you look at it now. Specify what for you makes it cringe-worthy.

145

DATE: _____

When you're sad, what could I say or do that would help you feel comforted?

_____
_____
_____
_____
_____
_____
_____
_____
_____

146

DATE: _____

Imagine that we lived in a place where the only self-expression permitted was through socks. Describe the different socks you might wear. If everyone was required to strip off their left sock at noon and trade it with someone, who would you avoid hanging out with midday?

_____
_____
_____
_____
_____

147

Which one of my friends do I seem to benefit most from in my life right now?

_____

_____

_____

_____

_____

_____

_____

_____

148

Which one of your friends do you sometimes think you could set better boundaries with?

_____

_____

_____

_____

_____

_____

_____

_____

_____

149

DATE: _____

What's one thing about me that you find adorable but have never told me about?

_____

_____

_____

_____

_____

_____

_____

_____

_____

150

DATE: _____

Do you believe in fate? If so, what do you think your fate might be? If not, why not?

_____

_____

_____

_____

_____

_____

_____

_____

_____

151 DATE: _____

In your view, who in my life could I open my heart to forgiving, and how might that be good for me?

_____

_____

_____

_____

_____

_____

_____

_____

152 DATE: _____

What do you think would make you more approachable to others? Is this a change you would want to make? Why or why not?

_____

_____

_____

_____

_____

_____

_____

_____

153
DATE: _____

What's one emotion other than joy or happiness you want to allow yourself to safely feel more frequently, and how will it help you be more authentically yourself?

_____

_____

_____

_____

_____

_____

_____

_____

154
DATE: _____

What's more important to you in a high-conflict situation: staying connected or asserting your convictions?

_____

_____

_____

_____

_____

_____

_____

_____

_____

155 DATE: _____

If I worked as a spy, what would be a great code name and cover story for me?

156 DATE: _____

Can you show me an old scar on your body, that I haven't noticed or paid much attention to, and tell me the story behind it? If I know about every one of your scars, is there a psychological or emotional scar I might not fully know about?

157 DATE: _____

If there were a historical cause you could participate in, which one would it be, and why?

158 DATE: _____

What's your ideal scenario of how I'd care for you when you're sick?

159 DATE: _____

How do you think about or interpret illness, and in what ways do those views help or hurt you when you get sick unexpectedly? Where did this view of illness originate?

---

160 DATE: _____

If I could have only one condiment to flavor my food for the rest of my life, what do you think I would choose, and how does that particular condiment reflect my personality?

---

161 DATE: _____

What inscription would be etched into our special love necklaces, bracelets, or rings (if we had them made today) that would capture the essence of our unique bond?

_____

_____

_____

_____

_____

_____

_____

_____

162 DATE: _____

How did your most valuable grade school friendship support you?

_____

_____

_____

_____

_____

_____

_____

_____

_____

163

DATE: _____

What song reminds you most of me, and why? (No wedding-day songs allowed.)

_____

_____

_____

_____

_____

_____

_____

_____

_____

164

DATE: _____

If your futuristic closet had only one nanofiber outfit in it that automatically adjusted to meet your functional clothing needs, would you feel relieved, or would you miss expressing yourself through how you dress? What do your sartorial choices communicate about you to the world?

_____

_____

_____

_____

_____

_____

Q165 DATE: _____

If you were in control of evolution, what extra ability would you give humans, and why?

_____

_____

_____

_____

_____

_____

_____

_____

_____

Q166 DATE: _____

What do you think was (or is) your family's darkest secret?

_____

_____

_____

_____

_____

_____

_____

_____

167

DATE: _____

Describe your biggest dream.

168

DATE: _____

What's holding you back from fully pursuing your biggest dream right now? What small steps can you take toward pursuing this dream?

169

DATE: _____

Name your favorite drink. When you smell it, what does it evoke?

_____

_____

_____

_____

_____

_____

_____

_____

_____

170

DATE: _____

If you had to live in a multiplayer video game of your own creation for one year, describe the kind of game you'd need to live in so you would stay grounded in reality.

_____

_____

_____

_____

_____

_____

_____

_____

171

If you could offer me a mantra or a phrase that you think would help keep my spirits up when I'm discouraged, what would it be?

172

What's the most meaningful gift you've ever received, and why?

173 DATE: _____

Tell me the words you'd like to say and truly believe on your deathbed. Why are those words meaningful to you?

_____

_____

_____

_____

_____

_____

_____

_____

_____

174 DATE: _____

What's something you hate now that you'd be willing to try again in 10 years?

_____

_____

_____

_____

_____

_____

_____

_____

175 DATE: _____

What three objects remind you of me the most, and why?

176 DATE: _____

Is it harder for you to multitask or singletask, and why?
How might practicing the harder one serve you and/or us as
a couple?

177

During an intense storm, how do you feel? Fearful? Excited? Soothed? Do your emotions come from a past experience?

_____

_____

_____

_____

_____

_____

_____

_____

178

What daily activity helps you stay optimistic, and how/why does that work?

_____

_____

_____

_____

_____

_____

_____

_____

_____

179 DATE: _____

What food or drink would you most enjoy bathing in?
Describe how it might feel for the two of us to bathe in
that substance.

180 DATE: _____

What's most enjoyable for you about the time we spend
together?

181 DATE: _____

Do you feel like you need more space in a relationship to feel safe, or more connection and closeness—and why do you think that is?

_____
_____
_____
_____
_____
_____
_____
_____

182 DATE: _____

Describe a time when you observed me carefully without my knowledge and felt positive feelings toward me.

_____
_____
_____
_____
_____
_____
_____
_____
_____

183 DATE: _____

Can you describe one thing I did this week
that you felt genuinely grateful for?

_____

_____

_____

_____

_____

_____

_____

184 DATE: _____

What was one of our hottest moments together when we
first met?

_____

_____

_____

_____

_____

_____

_____

_____

185 DATE: _____

What do you take most for granted in your life that you'd like to appreciate more: your friends, your job, your health, your wealth, your intelligence, or something else?

_____

_____

_____

_____

_____

_____

_____

_____

186 DATE: _____

Which one of these responses might help and which might make things worse if we were having a disagreement that was escalating? (1) I say, "Even though we're arguing, I want you to know I love you. Let's take a hug break." (2) I say, "I need to calm down; I'll be back," and walk out of the room. (3) I close my eyes, sit still, and take 20 slow, conscious breaths.

_____

_____

_____

_____

187 DATE: _____

If you have a long commute to work, what luxury would you give up to have a shorter one? If you have a short commute, what luxury would you sacrifice it for?

_____
_____
_____
_____
_____
_____
_____
_____

188 DATE: _____

If we were stuck standing up in a closet that was rigged to open at the peak of our mutual turn-on, what kind of foreplay would we engage in to open the door within five minutes?

_____
_____
_____
_____
_____
_____

189

DATE: _____

Who do you think taught you to celebrate life when you were growing up, and how?

_____

_____

_____

_____

_____

_____

_____

_____

_____

190

DATE: _____

If you could write a letter to the person who, in your view, made the biggest positive impact on me, whom would you write it to, and what would the letter say?

_____

_____

_____

_____

_____

_____

_____

191 DATE: _____

Tell me the one thing you criticize *most* in other people and what you think your deeper need or longing is underneath your criticisms.

---

192 DATE: _____

What world record for longest couples activity do you think we'd be best at setting: holding hands, kissing, engaging in foreplay, laughing, savoring amazing food, or cuddling in bed?

---

193 DATE: _____

What question could I ask you when we reconnect at the end of the day that would help you feel relaxed, accepted, and welcomed?

_____

_____

_____

_____

_____

_____

_____

_____

194 DATE: _____

From last year's New Year's Eve until now, how have you grown or changed?

_____

_____

_____

_____

_____

_____

_____

_____

195 DATE: _____

If you live to be 100 years old, what experience do you think you'd never get tired of?

_____

_____

_____

_____

_____

_____

_____

_____

196 DATE: _____

You gather your favorite people, living and/or dead, in one room for a night of fun. Who are they, and how do you imagine the night progressing?

_____

_____

_____

_____

_____

_____

_____

_____

197

DATE: _____

Did you give up on a hobby you loved, like painting, drawing, writing, rock climbing, hockey, tennis, ballroom dancing, or piano lessons, when you were young? What keeps you from starting up this hobby again now?

198

DATE: _____

What would you want me to do to support you during a medical procedure?

199 DATE: _____

What can you learn from my family traditions or culture, and what can I learn from yours?

_____
_____
_____
_____
_____
_____
_____
_____
_____

200 DATE: _____

Spiritually, how would you like to grow or expand to be more inclusive in your views of other people and of life in general?

_____
_____
_____
_____
_____
_____
_____
_____
_____
_____

201 DATE: _____

What's a quality you're looking for now when you make new friends that you didn't look for in your old friends?

_____
_____
_____
_____
_____
_____
_____
_____
_____

202 DATE: _____

Describe your ideal alien abduction experience; what do you learn from it that helps you live a fuller life when you return to this planet?

_____
_____
_____
_____
_____
_____
_____
_____

203 DATE: _____

What were you most attracted to in me when we first met,
and why is this trait or quality important to you in a partner?

204 DATE: _____

If you could write a heartfelt letter to an old friend you've lost
touch with but really care about, what would it say?

205 DATE: _____

Do you think you're mostly a stubborn person or mostly a flexible person, and what are the pros and cons of the way you are?

_____

_____

_____

_____

_____

_____

_____

206 DATE: _____

What activities make you feel sexy from the inside out (e.g., acing a presentation, killing it on the tennis court, taking a bath with music and candles, etc.)?

_____

_____

_____

_____

_____

_____

_____

207 DATE: _____

How does it feel when we sit together in silence and just look at each other? Can we do it now and then honestly describe the experience?

_____
_____
_____
_____
_____
_____
_____
_____

208 DATE: _____

What positive behaviors could I engage in that would make a dinner out with me feel more romantic (phrased as a do-able action, e.g., "Hold my hand," vs. "Don't be distant")?

_____
_____
_____
_____
_____
_____
_____
_____

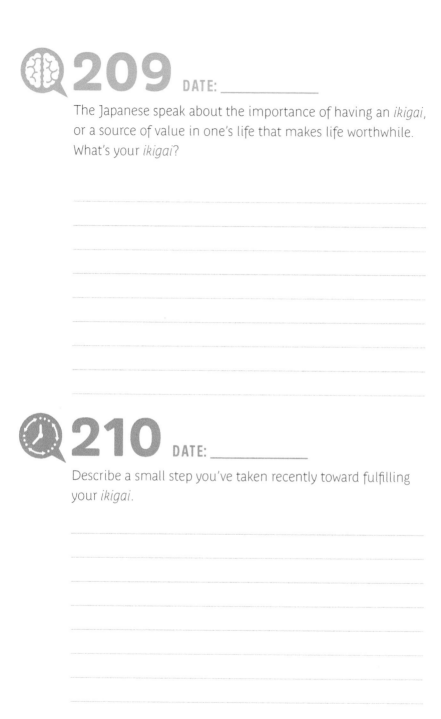

209

DATE: _____

The Japanese speak about the importance of having an *ikigai*, or a source of value in one's life that makes life worthwhile. What's your *ikigai*?

210

DATE: _____

Describe a small step you've taken recently toward fulfilling your *ikigai*.

211

DATE: _____

If we hosted a party together and decided to go "all out" (no limits), how do you envision it unfolding?

_____

_____

_____

_____

_____

_____

_____

212

DATE: _____

What's your least favorite season of the year, and why?

_____

_____

_____

_____

_____

_____

_____

_____

_____

_____

213 DATE: _____

What would you most enjoy hearing me say to others as I brag about you?

_____

_____

_____

_____

_____

_____

_____

_____

_____

214 DATE: _____

Can you remember an unexpectedly funny moment you witnessed or experienced that makes you smile or chuckle now?

_____

_____

_____

_____

_____

_____

_____

_____

_____

_____

215 DATE:_____

Is there a dark-ish secret you've buried away that you could risk sharing with me?

216 DATE:_____

What's one vision for the future you're pretty sure we share?

217 DATE: _____

If we were to grow old together, where geographically do you envision us having the best quality of life, and what would we be doing?

218 DATE: _____

Describe one random act of kindness you consciously engaged in today or this week; how did it feel to do that?

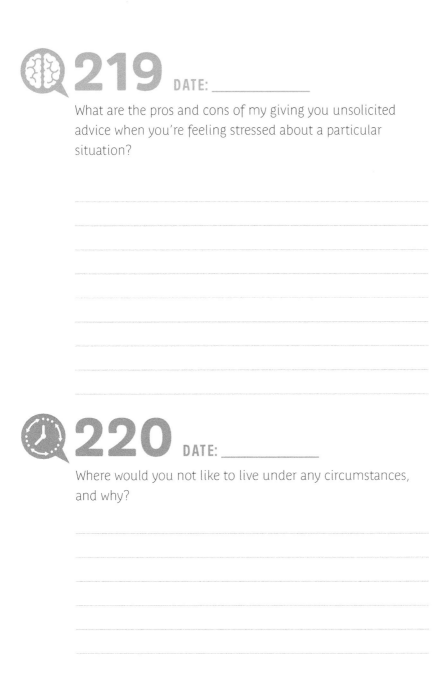

219 DATE: _____

What are the pros and cons of my giving you unsolicited advice when you're feeling stressed about a particular situation?

220 DATE: _____

Where would you not like to live under any circumstances, and why?

221 DATE: _____

What do you appreciate about my best friend, and why?

_____

_____

_____

_____

_____

_____

_____

_____

_____

222 DATE: _____

What's one small action you might find it easy to do a little more of daily to increase our affection for each other?

_____

_____

_____

_____

_____

_____

_____

_____

_____

223 DATE: _____

What do you like or dislike about sharing a bathroom with me (or the idea of it, if we don't share bathrooms)?

_____

_____

_____

_____

_____

_____

_____

_____

224 DATE: _____

Which of these dares is hardest, and why?
(1) write me an emoji-only love letter;
(2) communicate with me for 30 minutes with only grunts and facial expressions; or
(3) tie our shoelaces together and walk around the block.

_____

_____

_____

_____

225

DATE: _____

Is there something we can do in your least favorite season to enjoy it more?

_____

_____

_____

_____

_____

_____

_____

_____

226

DATE: _____

Some religions, such as Hinduism and Buddhism, include the doctrines of karma and reincarnation. These have been interpreted to mean our souls choose our caregivers before we're born in order to learn the lessons we need in this life. Given your experiences, how do you feel about that idea? What's it like for you to imagine this idea as a possibility?

_____

_____

_____

_____

_____

227 DATE: _____

What's one thing that's kept you tossing and turning in bed at night, in the recent past?

_____
_____
_____
_____
_____
_____
_____
_____
_____

228 DATE: _____

Is there someplace outdoors that you would love for us to have a picnic, and what would we bring and do to make it even more fun?

_____
_____
_____
_____
_____
_____
_____
_____

229

DATE: _____

Describe the psychological defenses you use most frequently to avoid emotional pain (minimizing, rationalizing, suppression, projection, etc.).

_____

_____

_____

_____

_____

_____

_____

230

DATE: _____

Our car breaks down at night in the wilderness and our cell phones die. Describe something new and fun for both of us that we might do to pass the time till morning (other than sleep).

_____

_____

_____

_____

_____

_____

231 DATE: _____

Which is harder for you, and why: admitting when you're wrong or sticking to your guns on something you really believe in?

_____

_____

_____

_____

_____

_____

_____

_____

232 DATE: _____

What makes it difficult to apologize when you've said or done something you regret? If you apologize too easily, what makes it hard for you to refrain from apologizing?

_____

_____

_____

_____

_____

_____

_____

_____

233 DATE: _____

When we disagree on something (such as musical preferences, a potential vacation spot, or our assessment of another
person), are you comfortable accepting our two distinct
views, or do you need to find (or negotiate) a zone of overlap
between our views to feel connected to me?

234 DATE: _____

What specific gesture or act of physical affection do you most
enjoy from me (hand holding, hair caressing, hugging, back
scratching, massage)?

235 DATE: _____

What book do you think we'd get a lot out of reading together?

_____

_____

_____

_____

_____

_____

_____

_____

236 DATE: _____

If you could institute a new national holiday honoring a thing, idea, or activity that's important to you, what would it be? Why and how do *you* value it?

_____

_____

_____

_____

_____

_____

_____

237 DATE: _____

Is it hard or easy for you to let me take control in small ways, like driving you someplace or making decisions about furniture, movies, restaurants, etc.? Why?

_____
_____
_____
_____
_____
_____
_____
_____
_____

238 DATE: _____

Would you enjoy or dread making a commitment to doing a silly thing together, like spraying each other with shaving cream in the shower or dressing up for Halloween on a non-Halloween day?

_____
_____
_____
_____
_____
_____
_____

239

DATE: _____

Do you believe it's better to ask for forgiveness or permission, and why?

240

DATE: _____

What movie would you like us to see together that would help me understand something important about you, and what should I look for as we watch it?

241 DATE: _____

What authority figure supported you most on the playgrounds or school hallways of your childhood or adolescence? How? If you didn't experience a protective authority figure, in what way did you support yourself through tough social moments where you were ignored, bullied, or left out?

_____

_____

_____

_____

_____

_____

_____

242 DATE: _____

What could turn one of our lukewarm reconnections into a "hot" moment?

_____

_____

_____

_____

_____

_____

_____

_____

_____

243 DATE: _____

How would you describe the quality of your ongoing inner dialogue with yourself: friendly, neutral, or critical? How does it impact us as a couple?

_____

_____

_____

_____

_____

_____

_____

_____

244 DATE: _____

What would you love for me to bring you for breakfast in bed in the morning if timing, money, and effort weren't a hindrance?

_____

_____

_____

_____

_____

_____

245
DATE: _____

What would your favorite surprise party entail?

_____
_____
_____
_____
_____
_____
_____
_____
_____
_____

246
DATE: _____

What ability or skill do you wish your parents had encouraged you to master as a child, and why?

_____
_____
_____
_____
_____
_____
_____
_____
_____
_____

247 DATE: _____

What skill or ability did your parents encourage you to master as a child that you resisted but are now grateful you learned?

248 DATE: _____

Give me an example of a time or situation when embarrassment or shame impacted your ability to communicate your feelings (with me or with someone else) and ask for what you needed.

249 DATE: _____

What physical issue or symptom (like migraines, digestive issues, or back pain) have you struggled with that might have a psychological component or be connected to a past emotional event?

_____

_____

_____

_____

_____

_____

_____

250 DATE: _____

What piece of jewelry do you wear (or did you once wear) that reflects some important part of your personality?
In what way?

_____

_____

_____

_____

_____

_____

_____

_____

251 DATE: _____

What would be a grand gesture of love you might enjoy experiencing, and why?

_____

_____

_____

_____

_____

_____

_____

_____

252 DATE: _____

If we recorded our own "kitchen song" using pots, pans, glasses, and spoons, what would you enjoy and/or fear about sharing the song on social media or somewhere else? Can we try creating a kitchen song, even if we don't share it?

_____

_____

_____

_____

_____

_____

253

In general, how do you like me to perceive you?

_____

_____

_____

_____

_____

_____

_____

_____

_____

_____

254

If you and I went to the gym together (or if we already do), what would (or do) you enjoy most about going through a workout routine with me?

_____

_____

_____

_____

_____

_____

_____

_____

_____

255

DATE: _____

Can you describe the most foolish thing you think you've ever done in your life?

_____

_____

_____

_____

_____

_____

_____

_____

_____

256

DATE: _____

What's an activity you thought you hated but then tried and liked?

_____

_____

_____

_____

_____

_____

_____

_____

257 DATE: _____

We're in a hot air balloon and it starts leaking—what would you want me to know about you or us that I don't already know as we descend (hopefully safely)?

_____

_____

_____

_____

_____

_____

_____

_____

258 DATE: _____

What are my unique, subtle "happy signals," or the almost imperceptible signs that I'm open and relaxed?

_____

_____

_____

_____

_____

_____

_____

_____

259 DATE: _____

If you could make one thing legal that's illegal and one thing illegal that's legal where you/we live, what would these things be, and why?

260 DATE: _____

Name one self-destructive action you took in your teenage years that you wish you could reverse. Imagine symbolically undoing it now and describe how that feels.

261 DATE: _____

If you were an artist and I were your model, what materials would you require to immortalize my unique appeal most effectively?

_____
_____
_____
_____
_____
_____
_____
_____

262 DATE: _____

What's one difficult, emotional conversation you've been dreading having with someone important in your personal or professional life, and why is it scary?

_____
_____
_____
_____
_____
_____
_____

263 DATE: _____

For that scary conversation you mentioned in question 262, can you briefly act out both parts of how the conversation would unfold in a best-case scenario?

264 DATE: _____

Would there be a downside to us always being happy together, never having conflicts, agreeing on almost everything, and seeing life the same way? If this is already us, what are the pros and cons of being so content and similar?

265 DATE: _____

Who are you still struggling to forgive in your life, and how did they hurt you?

_____
_____
_____
_____
_____
_____
_____
_____
_____

266 DATE: _____

Can you tune in to your "inner critic radio station" and impersonate your radio host's voice?

_____
_____
_____
_____
_____
_____
_____
_____

267 DATE: _____

What's one simple thing that could reduce your level of irritability in our relationship (e.g., sleeping eight hours; drinking less alcohol; forgoing white flour, sugar, processed food, nicotine, and/or caffeine; drinking more water; exercising), and what interferes with doing it?

268 DATE: _____

What's one memory we share that you think means a lot to both of us?

269

DATE: _____

On your life graph, how do you think the overall pattern has changed over the years when you look at the high highs, the low lows, and everything in between?

_____

_____

_____

_____

_____

_____

_____

_____

270

DATE: _____

How would you describe my sense of humor, and how does it make you feel when one of us makes the other laugh really hard?

_____

_____

_____

_____

_____

_____

_____

_____

271 DATE: _____

What are three things I do for you on a regular basis that other people might not know about?

272 DATE: _____

Do you think there's a difference between secrecy and privacy, and if so, what is it?

273

DATE: _____

What household, financial, social, or other decisions are you a little anxious to consult with me about, and what could I do to reduce your anxiety?

_____

_____

_____

_____

_____

_____

_____

_____

274

DATE: _____

What's my body language when I'm frustrated? Describe how your body responds to my frustration when you sense it.

_____

_____

_____

_____

_____

_____

_____

_____

275 DATE: _____

Can you tell me about whether you think it would feel good or uncomfortable if I wrote you a love letter (or e-mail) daily for one week?

_____

_____

_____

_____

_____

_____

_____

_____

276 DATE: _____

What's the first idea that comes into your mind for a silly home movie we could make together?

_____

_____

_____

_____

_____

_____

_____

_____

_____

277 DATE: _____

What's your biggest hope for us individually and as a couple?

_____
_____
_____
_____
_____
_____
_____
_____
_____
_____

278 DATE: _____

Can you describe in detail one of my favorite meals currently, or guess at it?

_____
_____
_____
_____
_____
_____
_____

279

If we were to live on the first prototype of a floating city, what do you think would be some pros and cons of living there?

280

If you had to inhale one smell for all eternity, what smell would you want it to be, and why don't you think you'd get sick of it?

281 DATE: _____

Describe the room you spent most of your time in as a child. What feelings, thoughts, or memories come to you as you describe it?

_____
_____
_____
_____
_____
_____
_____
_____

282 DATE: _____

What kind of outfit do you think I like to see you dressed up in the most?

_____
_____
_____
_____
_____
_____
_____
_____
_____

283 DATE: _____

What was one of the wisest choices you've ever made in your life?

_____

_____

_____

_____

_____

_____

_____

_____

284 DATE: _____

If you had to have a nickname, what would you want to be called, and why?

_____

_____

_____

_____

_____

_____

_____

_____

285 DATE: _____

What would be some new ways of expressing myself (verbally, or through music, writing, movement, or touch) that I could learn that might thrill or delight you?

286 DATE: _____

What is the scariest experience you've had outdoors, away from society, and how do you think it might have impacted your view of nature?

287 DATE: _____

Would you rather be a creative genius who was perceived in your lifetime as mediocre, or be mediocre but perceived in your lifetime as a creative genius? Why?

_____

_____

_____

_____

_____

_____

_____

_____

288 DATE: _____

What does it feel like in all parts of your body to kiss me very, very slowly? Are you open to kissing for a minute to help us answer this question correctly?

_____

_____

_____

_____

_____

_____

_____

289 DATE: _____

Is there a form of affection you really crave that I don't give you enough of, and who may have given (or failed to give) you this affection in your childhood?

_____

_____

_____

_____

_____

_____

_____

_____

290 DATE: _____

If we played with dominant/submissive roles for one hour, which role would you feel most and least comfortable in? Why?

_____

_____

_____

_____

_____

_____

_____

_____

291 DATE: _____

Do you prefer fooling around with clothes on, partially on, or all off, and why?

_____

_____

_____

_____

_____

_____

_____

_____

292 DATE: _____

What memories come to mind when you think of your first car (or bicycle)?

_____

_____

_____

_____

_____

_____

_____

 **293** DATE: _____

What's one quirky facial expression I sometimes
make that you've noticed, and what do you think
I'm expressing when I make it?

_____

_____

_____

_____

_____

_____

_____

_____

294 DATE: _____

What emotional wound in me do you wish you could heal,
and why?

_____

_____

_____

_____

_____

_____

_____

_____

_____

295 DATE: _____

What would you most enjoy as a way of reconnecting after a day apart: a six-second hug, the words "I'm happy to see you," or some other action/greeting?

296 DATE: _____

Can you tell me honestly about one sexual fantasy you've had about me that you haven't shared with me yet because you've felt too shy?

297

DATE: _____

What aspect of your professional life do you struggle with most, and why?

_____

_____

_____

_____

_____

_____

_____

_____

_____

_____

298

DATE: _____

What elements would our ideal day together include to satisfy your deepest desires for acceptance, joy, connection, and fun?

_____

_____

_____

_____

_____

_____

_____

_____

299

DATE: _____

What breaks your heart about being human? How do you think this heartbreak might also open you up to others?

_____

_____

_____

_____

_____

_____

_____

_____

300

DATE: _____

Where could we make out and/or feel each other up that would be naughty?

_____

_____

_____

_____

_____

_____

_____

_____

_____

301

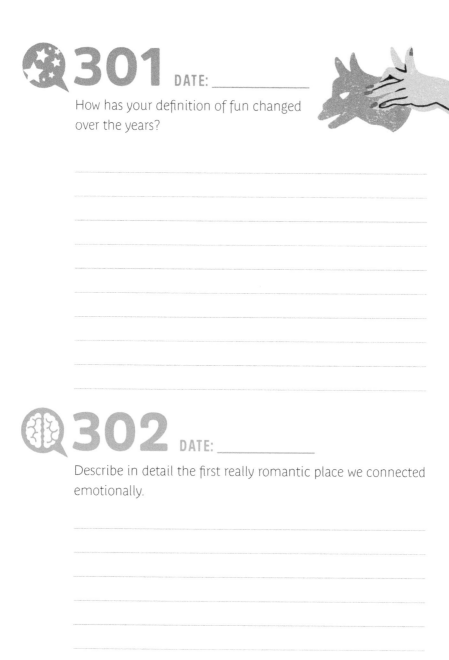

DATE: _____

How has your definition of fun changed over the years?

_____

_____

_____

_____

_____

_____

_____

_____

_____

302

DATE: _____

Describe in detail the first really romantic place we connected emotionally.

_____

_____

_____

_____

_____

_____

_____

_____

_____

303

DATE: _____

How did you feel around my family when you met them for the first time?

_____

_____

_____

_____

_____

_____

_____

_____

304

DATE: _____

What was the biggest life lesson you've learned from one of your failures or successes?

_____

_____

_____

_____

_____

_____

_____

_____

_____

_____

305

DATE: _____

What was the hardest or most surprising thing about meeting one of my exes or coming across an "ex" memento?

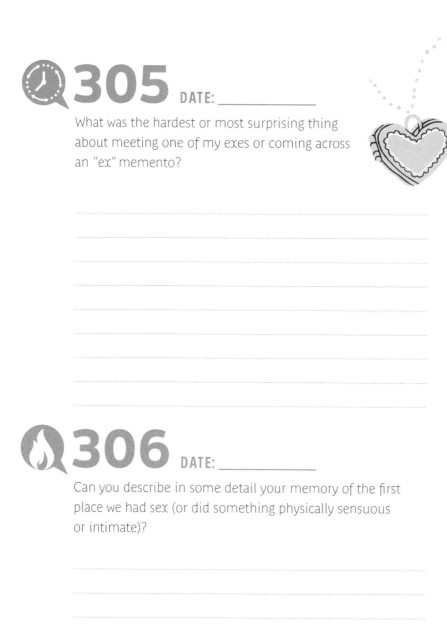

_____

_____

_____

_____

_____

_____

_____

_____

306

DATE: _____

Can you describe in some detail your memory of the first place we had sex (or did something physically sensuous or intimate)?

_____

_____

_____

_____

_____

_____

_____

_____

307

DATE: _____

When was the first time you realized I had longer-term potential as a partner?

_____

_____

_____

_____

_____

_____

_____

_____

308

DATE: _____

If you could invent and patent a new product, would it be something that would entertain people or something that would serve a practical purpose?

_____

_____

_____

_____

_____

_____

_____

_____

309 DATE: _____

What do you consider one of the most fascinating or unusual things about me?

_____

_____

_____

_____

_____

_____

_____

_____

_____

310 DATE: _____

Describe a striking outfit I wore when we first dated or met, and what you made of it.

_____

_____

_____

_____

_____

_____

_____

_____

311 DATE: _____

Would you rather be rich and famous or rich and anonymous, and why?

_____

_____

_____

_____

_____

_____

_____

_____

312 DATE: _____

What does it feel like when you need or want something from me, and you ask me for it directly with no guarantee that I'll give it to you?

_____

_____

_____

_____

_____

_____

_____

313 DATE: _____

What's an uncommon profession you might like to experience for a day, and what do you imagine you'd learn or gain from the experience (e.g., bounty hunter, professional bridesmaid, hacker waterslide tester)?

_____

_____

_____

_____

_____

_____

_____

314 DATE: _____

If you could dress like a movie icon of the gender other than the one you identify with, who would it be, and why?

_____

_____

_____

_____

_____

_____

_____

_____

315 DATE: _____

If you could envision an inner circle of people to boost your spirits when you lack confidence, which people would you choose? Why them?

316 DATE: _____

With whom do you think I collaborate best on things I'm passionate about, and why?

317

DATE: _____

Describe your biggest financial mistake and the silver lining.

_____

_____

_____

_____

_____

_____

_____

_____

_____

_____

_____

318

DATE: _____

Have you ever gotten rid of something that was given to you by a person you cared about, which you now wish you'd kept? If so, why do you regret it? If not, what is something you've held on to that you probably could or should let go of?

_____

_____

_____

_____

_____

_____

_____

319 DATE: _____

What are some of the mundane tasks you consider tedious, overly time-consuming, or uninteresting that you wouldn't mind robots doing for you in the future? What would be a downside to no longer doing those mundane tasks?

_____

_____

_____

_____

_____

_____

_____

320 DATE: _____

What do you do with your friends that you wish you could do with me?

_____

_____

_____

_____

_____

_____

_____

_____

321

DATE: _____

What do you think would be the hardest part for you about going on a three-day, no-technology, silent retreat together?

322

DATE: _____

When you imagine yourself in 10 years, how have you changed as a person? How have you *not* changed?

323 DATE: _____

Can you describe the most extreme emergency situation you've ever been in and how you handled it?

324 DATE: _____

If you had to eat something that you found revolting, what visualization or other mindfulness practice might help you get through it? Can you tell me something you would never want to eat and then mime the experience of eating it for me now?

325 DATE: _____

What's the most rebellious act you've ever engaged in?

_____

_____

_____

_____

_____

_____

_____

_____

_____

_____

326 DATE: _____

If telepathy were possible, what's a situation when being able to read each other's minds (with consent) might help our relationship?

_____

_____

_____

_____

_____

_____

_____

_____

_____

327 DATE: _____

Who's currently your most and least favorite relative, and why?

_____

_____

_____

_____

_____

_____

_____

_____

328 DATE: _____

What has been your most formative "in the spotlight" experience?

_____

_____

_____

_____

_____

_____

_____

_____

_____

 **329** DATE: _____

Do you think you sometimes protect your heart from the risk of loving or feeling deeply? If so, why, and in what ways?

_____

_____

_____

_____

_____

_____

_____

330 DATE: _____

If you and I could learn a partnered dance together, what would it be, and how do you think learning it would challenge us and/or bring us closer?

_____

_____

_____

_____

_____

_____

_____

331 DATE: _____

If we are still alive when medical nanorobots are able to fix our ailing cells and allow us to live to be 150 years old, how might we need to rethink our views of a lifelong romantic commitment?

_____
_____
_____
_____
_____
_____
_____
_____
_____

332 DATE: _____

What mythical or legendary hero do you most relate to, and why?

_____
_____
_____
_____
_____
_____
_____
_____
_____
_____

333 DATE: _____

What's one situation in the past when you felt torn between doing what was right and doing what was convenient? How did you resolve that dilemma?

334 DATE: _____

If you had $250,000 to invest in any company that you think will be hugely successful in 10 years, what would that company produce or do?

335

DATE: _____

When you see someone texting and driving, what thoughts go through your head? How do you imagine they rationalize this behavior? What's one risky behavior you've rationalized in the past?

_____
_____
_____
_____
_____
_____
_____
_____
_____

336

DATE: _____

Have you ever spent 24 hours completely naked? What was (or would be) fun about that, and what was (or would be) not so fun?

_____
_____
_____
_____
_____
_____
_____
_____

337
DATE: _____

What has been a peak erotic experience you've had with me?

_____
_____
_____
_____
_____
_____
_____
_____
_____

338
DATE: _____

Are there more advantages or more disadvantages, in your view, to staying connected to people who have been important to you but are difficult to be around?

_____
_____
_____
_____
_____
_____
_____
_____

339

DATE: _____

In general, when people offer you something you're not expecting, is your natural impulse to accept their offering or to turn it down? Why do you think that is?

340

DATE: _____

Describe the moment you first realized you'd reached adulthood. If you haven't had that moment yet, how do you envision it feeling when (or if) it arrives?

341 DATE: _____

Can you paint a picture, in words, of your mother (figure)'s or father (figure)'s face?

_____

_____

_____

_____

_____

_____

_____

_____

342 DATE: _____

What business is our/your neighborhood most in need of, and how do you think it would improve our quality of life if such a business opened within walking distance of our/your home?

_____

_____

_____

_____

_____

_____

343 DATE: _____

If you were running for political office, what would your campaign slogan be and what would be some of your main talking points?

_____

_____

_____

_____

_____

_____

_____

_____

344 DATE: _____

What's the most humorous situation we were ever involved in together that didn't seem humorous when it was happening? What makes it funny now?

_____

_____

_____

_____

_____

_____

_____

_____

345 DATE: _____

Who was your favorite celebrity growing up, and what is or was it about them that you liked or found inspiring?

_____

_____

_____

_____

_____

_____

_____

_____

346 DATE: _____

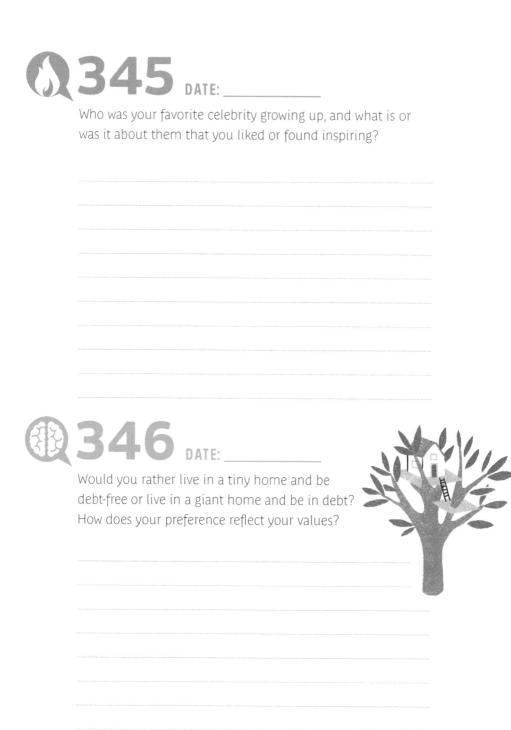

Would you rather live in a tiny home and be debt-free or live in a giant home and be in debt? How does your preference reflect your values?

_____

_____

_____

_____

_____

_____

347 DATE: _____

Where did you like to shop as a young adult, and why?

_____

_____

_____

_____

_____

_____

_____

_____

_____

_____

348 DATE: _____

Would you rather tour America in an RV for two weeks, spend two weeks in an Italian villa, or go on a two-week luxury cruise, and why?

_____

_____

_____

_____

_____

_____

_____

_____

_____

349 DATE: _____

Which holiday makes you feel most unsettled, and why?

_____

_____

_____

_____

_____

_____

_____

_____

_____

_____

350 DATE: _____

If you could make a documentary that millions of people saw across the world, what theme would you focus on to make the biggest positive global impact?

_____

_____

_____

_____

_____

_____

_____

_____

_____

351 DATE: _____

What's your most and least favorite
mode of transportation, and why?

_____

_____

_____

_____

_____

_____

_____

_____

_____

352 DATE: _____

If we traded routines for a day, what part of my routine do
you imagine you'd find relaxing, pleasurable, or exciting, and
what do you think you'd struggle with?

_____

_____

_____

_____

_____

_____

_____

_____

353 DATE: _____

When you were a child, did someone sing to you, read you stories, or help you through a goodnight ritual? If so, what details of that process do you remember? If not, did you create your own?

_____

_____

_____

_____

_____

_____

_____

_____

354 DATE: _____

If you could rewrite one of the most painful chapters of your life with a new ending, what would that ending be? If you've already rewritten it, how do you envision the happiest chapter of your life beginning?

_____

_____

_____

_____

_____

_____

_____

_____

355

DATE: _____

If you and I met at a costume ball incognito, what gesture, facial expression, habitual body language, or eccentricity would give me away as me?

_____

_____

_____

_____

_____

_____

_____

_____

356

DATE: _____

Which of your senses do you rely on most heavily? How might temporarily relying on one of your other senses help you connect with me in a new way?

_____

_____

_____

_____

_____

_____

_____

_____

357

DATE: _____

What was your favorite class in high school or college, and why?

_____
_____
_____
_____
_____
_____
_____
_____
_____

358

DATE: _____

What's the sickest you've ever been, and what did you learn from your illness?

_____
_____
_____
_____
_____
_____
_____
_____

359 DATE: _____

What's the nicest thing I've ever said to you or done for you?

_____

_____

_____

_____

_____

_____

_____

_____

_____

_____

360 DATE: _____

What car do you think reflects my personality, and why?

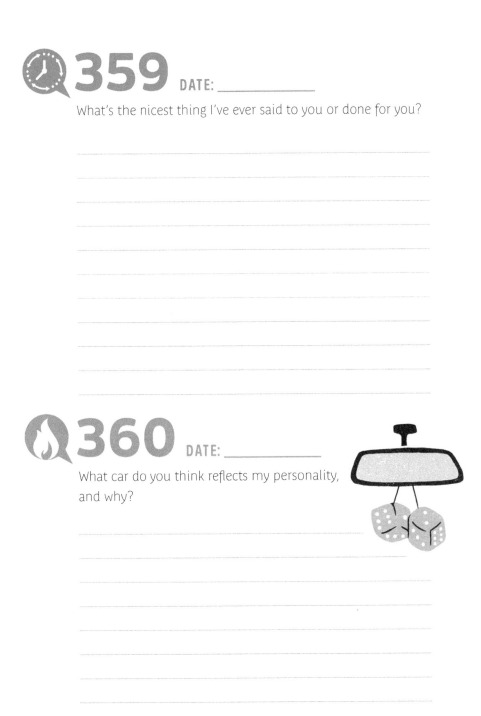

_____

_____

_____

_____

_____

_____

_____

_____

361 DATE: _____

Who in your family history do you feel a special connection to or wish you had met in person? Why do you feel that connection?

_____

_____

_____

_____

_____

_____

_____

_____

362 DATE: _____

Can you think of a problem you have right now that you might be able to "fix" just by surrendering to it and accepting it? How would that feel?

_____

_____

_____

_____

_____

_____

363 DATE: _____

Where do you think the balance is in a relationship between trying to please each other and trying to be authentic and true to oneself?

_____

_____

_____

_____

_____

_____

_____

_____

_____

364 DATE: _____

If I were going to rename you, I would name you
_____ because _____.

_____

_____

_____

_____

_____

_____

_____

_____

_____

_____

_____

 **365** DATE: _____

Describe your most memorable experience
of unconditional love.

_____

_____

_____

_____

_____

_____

_____

_____

_____

Year-Closer Reflection

You've traveled through this journal over the course of 365 days (give or take) and as many questions. You've peered into each other's pasts, gotten to know the intricacies of each other's presents, and seen into the future through one another's eyes. You've reflected, listened, shared, understood, wondered, and maybe also risked revealing aspects of yourself that you might typically dismiss, keep private, or avoid exploring altogether. At times, you've likely even dipped your toe—or maybe your entire foot—into deeper emotional and psychological undercurrents.

By coming back to these pages repeatedly, you've made your connection as a couple a priority. This journal isn't just a record of a *Love Ritual* you've engaged in over the course of a year—it's a testament to your willingness to go deeper. You've wondered, revealed, explored, and played together.

To conclude your *Year of Us* journey, answer the following five questions:

1. What was the most important thing you learned about yourself in this process?

2. What was the most memorable thing you learned about me?

3. What's a challenge you overcame working through this journal with me?

4. How has engaging in the *Year of Us* questions impacted how you see me, yourself, and our relationship?

5. How have I changed in the past year?

About the Author

Alicia Muñoz is a couples' therapist and the author of *No More Fighting: 20 Minutes a Week to a Stronger Relationship*. She earned her master's degree from New York University in mental health and wellness counseling, and her postgraduate certification in Imago Relationship Therapy. Prior to opening her private practice, Alicia provided individual, couples, and group therapy at Bellevue Hospital's World Trade Center Mental Health Program. Passionate about couplehood, Alicia shares her views on the power of committed love-partnerships on her blog, as well as in *Psychotherapy Networker*, *Counseling Today*, and on *The Good Men Project*. She lives in Virginia with her husband and son. You can follow her on Instagram at @aliciamunozcouples, on Twitter and Facebook at @aliciamunozlpc, and sign up for her newsletter at www.AliciaMunoz.com.